The Updated

JERUSALEM

Travel Guide 2023-2024

Discover the Timeless Treasures of
Jerusalem

Alanna Marrow

Table Of Contents

The Updated Jerusalem Travel Guide 2023-2024

Map Of Jerusalem

The Updated Jerusalem Travel Guide 2023-2024

Introduction

Welcome to a journey through the timeless and enchanting city of Jerusalem, where history and spirituality converge in a harmonious tapestry. As you hold this travel guide in your hands, you are about to embark on an unforgettable expedition through one of the world's most captivating destinations.

Jerusalem, a city of ancient origins and modern vibrancy, beckons travelers from all corners of the globe with its rich heritage, diverse cultures, and profound significance to three major religions—Judaism, Christianity, and Islam. With the utmost pleasure, we present to you the comprehensive Jerusalem Travel Guide for 2023-2024, meticulously curated to ensure your exploration is both seamless and rewarding.

Immerse yourself in the captivating atmosphere of the Old City, a UNESCO World Heritage Site, where labyrinthine streets unveil a treasure trove of sacred sites, bustling markets, and centuries-old architecture. Wander through its quarters—Jewish, Christian, Muslim, and Armenian—each encapsulates the essence of its respective community and offers glimpses into their timeless traditions.

This guide will lead you to the iconic Western Wall, a site of profound reverence and prayer for countless generations. Discover the resplendent Dome of the Rock, a pinnacle of Islamic architecture, standing gracefully atop the Temple Mount. Explore the solemn Church of the Holy Sepulchre, believed to encompass the crucifixion and burial sites of Jesus Christ, where pilgrims find solace and spiritual awakening.

Beyond its religious splendor, Jerusalem boasts a dynamic cultural scene, where contemporary art, music, and theater thrive. Engage in the vivacity of festivals and events, celebrating both ancient rituals and modern creativity. Delight your taste buds with the fusion of flavors that characterize Jerusalem's culinary landscape, from mouthwatering street food to fine dining experiences, and savor a feast that reflects the city's diverse heritage.

As you venture beyond the city's walls, you will find landscapes that resonate with tales of old—hike the hills that witnessed biblical narratives, float effortlessly in the mineral-rich waters of the Dead Sea, and uncover hidden oases in the arid wilderness.

Our guide extends its hand to assist you in practical matters, from navigating the city's transportation network to selecting the perfect accommodation that complements your journey. Be equipped with valuable tips to ensure your safety and seamless travel experience.

Jerusalem's allure is not limited to a single year; rather, it spans centuries, each generation inscribing its own stories into the city's enduring narrative. With a focus on sustainable tourism, we encourage you to engage with the community and contribute to the preservation of this remarkable heritage for future generations to cherish.

As you turn the pages of this travel guide, allow us to be your trusted companion, unveiling the layers of Jerusalem's splendor and guiding you on an expedition of profound significance. The 2023-2024 edition is an invitation to embrace the past, savor the present, and become a part of Jerusalem's ever-evolving tale.

May your journey be filled with discovery, wonder, and a deeper appreciation for the eternal city of Jerusalem.

Safe travels,

Chapter One

About Jerusalem

History

The ancient city of Jerusalem, which is rich in history and religious significance, serves as a metaphor for spirituality and human civilization. Its history spans millennia and is woven into a tapestry by numerous civilizations, religions, conquerors, and searchers of the truth. Jerusalem's history, from its modest beginnings to its current standing as a metropolis, is proof of the resilient human spirit.

Archaeological finds at surrounding sites show that the earliest signs of human occupation in the area around Jerusalem date to the 4th millennium BCE. The Canaanites, Jebusites, and Egyptians were among the ancient civilizations that eventually settled in the region and left their marks on the topography.

Jerusalem, however, rose to prominence in the reign of King David, circa 1000 BCE. The city was made the capital of the Confederate Kingdom of Israel after David's conquest, and King Solomon continued to administer it in that capacity. Jerusalem's history was forever changed when the First Temple was built atop the Temple Mount, becoming the hub of Jewish religious and cultural life.

With several invasions and conquests, the city's destiny underwent a significant change. King Nebuchadnezzar II of the Babylonian Empire conquered Jerusalem in 587 BCE, which resulted in the destruction of the First Temple and the exile of the Jewish people to Babylon. After several years, the Persians took control of the city, allowing the Jews to restore their revered temple.

Alexander the Great of Macedonia conquered the area in 333 BCE, introducing Hellenistic culture to Jerusalem. After his passing, the city was ruled by the Ptolemies and then the Seleucids. This was followed by a Jewish uprising headed by the Maccabees, which briefly restored the city's independence.

When the Roman Empire arrived in 63 BCE, Jerusalem was included in their expanding sphere of influence. With the construction of the Second Temple, which is renowned for its majesty, and subsequently, the turbulent Jewish-Roman wars, which culminated in the Second Temple's destruction in 70 CE, this era saw both grandeur and warfare.

Up to the 7th century, when the Islamic Caliphate under Umar ibn al-Khattab conquered Jerusalem, several empires, notably the Byzantine and Persian, rose and fell during the following centuries. Beginning with this,

Islam developed a strong bond with the city that eventually led to the Dome of the Rock and the Al-Aqsa Mosque being built on the Temple Mount.

Jerusalem was ruled by several Islamic dynasties throughout the Middle Ages, as well as Crusader nations during the Crusades. The Ottoman Empire triumphed in 1517, dominating Jerusalem for centuries up until the conclusion of World War I.

Jerusalem's history underwent a major transformation in the 20th century. Jerusalem became a focus of tension between the Arab and Jewish communities after World War I when the area was ruled by the British Mandate. Jerusalem was to be designated as an international city under the United Nations partition plan of 1947, but the subsequent conflict caused the city to be divided between Israel and Jordan.

Jerusalem was united with Israel after the 1967 Six-Day War, establishing Jerusalem's role as the nation's capital. Jerusalem continues to be a revered hub of religious travel and cross-cultural interaction despite the continuous difficulties and political obstacles.

Jerusalem still exists as a place where traditional practices and contemporary life coexist peacefully. The Western Wall, the Church of the Holy Sepulchre, and the Al-Aqsa Mosque are just a few of the historical and religious sites that continue to draw tourists from all over the world who are hoping to experience the timeless spirit that has created Jerusalem's extraordinary past. Even as the city changes, its heritage persists, serving as a constant reminder that Jerusalem is more than simply a physical location but also a metaphor for peace and the search for spiritual truth.

Culture

A city of great cultural significance, Jerusalem reflects a special fusion of history, religion, and traditions. Being one of the oldest cities in the world, it is home to a diverse tapestry of civilizations that have left their mark over many centuries.

Jerusalem's religious past is closely entwined with its culture. The city is a hub for pilgrims and spiritual seekers since it is home to holy places venerated by Jews, Christians, and Muslims alike. Among the respected sites of significant cultural and religious significance are the Western Wall, the Church of the Holy Sepulchre, and the Al-Aqsa Mosque.

Jerusalem's thriving arts and architecture reflect the many various influences it has encountered through conquests and settlements.

The city's cultural sector is thriving and active, encompassing both contemporary artistic manifestations and historic archaeological discoveries.

The food in Jerusalem is a feast for the senses, fusing flavors from many ethnicities. The city's cuisine reflects its cultural diversity, whether you're savoring traditional hummus and falafel in crowded markets or delving into sumptuous Middle Eastern delicacies in cozy restaurants.

The warmth and friendliness of the Jerusalem residents add to the city's distinctive cultural identity. The tenacity and durability of this historic city are demonstrated by the traditions and rituals that have been passed down through the years.

The cultural environment of Jerusalem is further enhanced by festivals and festivities. The city comes alive with music, dance, and joyful gatherings, joining individuals from many backgrounds, from religious observances to cultural activities.

Jerusalem's culture is essentially a complex tapestry of human history, religion, art, and creativity. It is a location where the past and present live in peace with one another and where guests are invited to immerse themselves in a world of intriguing experiences and timeless delights.

Geography

Jerusalem, a historic city perched on Judean Mountain hills, has a distinctive and alluring topography. It is a crossroads of continents and civilizations because it is situated in the Middle East.

Jerusalem has historically served as a hub for trade and conquest because of its advantageous location between the Dead Sea and the Mediterranean Sea to the east and west, respectively. The Mount of Olives, the city's highest peak and vantage point, provides spectacular panoramic views of the city below. The city's height varies.

Jerusalem's Old City, which is separated into four distinct quarters: the Jewish Quarter, Christian Quarter, Muslim Quarter, and Armenian Quarter, is the geographic center of the city. It is encircled by ominous walls. Narrow lanes leading to holy places and historic landmarks may be found in each neighborhood, each of which has its unique historical and religious significance.

Jerusalem's eastern border is formed by the Kidron Valley, which divides it from the Mount of Olives. The Valley of Hinnom, which combines with the Valley of the Tyropoeon in the center of the Old City, is located to the west.

These valleys give Jerusalem's topography depth and have been crucial to the city's growth throughout history.

Modern Jerusalem extends into a varied metropolitan landscape outside the Old City. The new city has thriving neighborhoods, green spaces, museums, and administrative buildings that symbolize the modern sides of this historic metropolis.

Jerusalem has a Mediterranean climate, which features warm, dry summers and chilly, rainy winters. The city has four unique seasons, and each one enhances the attractiveness of the area.

Jerusalem is a city of great religious significance, and its location has had a significant impact on its history and culture. Its religious places draw a large number of pilgrims and tourists, adding to its multicultural atmosphere.

Chapter Two

Planning your trip

Budgeting (how to save money)

Making wise decisions and careful planning are required when organizing a trip to Jerusalem on a budget. Here are some suggestions to help you get the most out of your trip without going over budget:

Travel Off-Peak: Think about going to Jerusalem in the spring or the autumn, when there are fewer tourists and lodging and travel costs are typically less expensive.

Flexible Vacation Dates: To benefit from lower airfare and lodging costs, be flexible with your vacation dates. To find the best prices, use websites that compare fares.

Instead of luxurious hotels, consider more affordable lodging options like hostels, guesthouses, or vacation rentals. It can potentially be less expensive to stay away from the city center.

Public Transportation: Save money by using Jerusalem's effective public transportation system, which includes buses and light rail, to travel across the city and its surrounding areas.

City Passes: Think about buying a city pass or attraction card, which frequently provides discounted or free admission to well-known attractions, museums, and public transportation.

Take advantage of the city's numerous free attractions, including the Western Wall, the Church of the Holy Sepulchre, and the crowded markets of the Old City.

Local Restaurants: Enjoy real cuisine at lower costs than tourist-oriented restaurants by dining at neighborhood restaurants and markets.

Water: To avoid purchasing bottled water, carry a refillable water bottle and fill it up at public fountains.

Guided Tours: To see the city's landmarks without incurring additional costs, select self-guided tours or sign up for no-cost walking tours.

Negotiate: To get better rates on presents and souvenirs when shopping in marketplaces or souks, don't be afraid to haggle over costs.

When to visit

The ideal time to travel to Jerusalem depends on personal tastes and the type of experience desired. You can use the following factors to select when to start your trip planning:

March to May:

The warm temperatures of spring in Jerusalem make it the perfect season for outdoor activities and sightseeing. Gardens and parks throughout the city are in full bloom, giving the area a lovely feel. Easter and Passover celebrations also take place around this time, enhancing the experience with further ethnic diversity.

September to November:

Autumn offers warm weather and fewer tourists than spring. It's a delightful time to explore the city and its surroundings as the scenery changes with the arrival of the magnificent autumn colors. Jewish holidays like Sukkot and Rosh Hashanah are observed in the autumn, giving your trip a cultural edge.

Summertime (June through August)

Jerusalem's summer months can be hot and dry, but they also coincide with the busiest travel period.

While there are many festivals and the city is bustling, there may be crowds and higher lodging costs. If you can tolerate the heat, you may still take advantage of the lively atmosphere and many daytime hours.

December through February is winter.

Although Jerusalem has mild winters, it can sometimes feel chilly, especially at night. Due to the low tourist season, you can anticipate fewer crowds and possibly better lodging prices. Winter may be a calm and cost-effective time to discover the city's historical and cultural treasures if you don't mind the chilly weather.

Religious Events:

If you want to experience distinctive traditions and celebrations, think about going when there are big religious occasions. As an illustration, Easter draws visitors to the Holy Sepulchre, and Ramadan, the Muslim holy month, offers a unique cultural experience.

How to visit

Jerusalem is easily accessible by a variety of transport options, making travel there reasonably simple. The most popular ways to go to this wonderful city are listed below:

1. By Air: Ben Gurion Airport (TLV), which is in Tel Aviv and is about 40 km west of Jerusalem, is the closest international airport. You can go to Jerusalem in about 45 minutes via direct airport express rail, private shuttle, or cab from the airport.

2. By Train: Israel Railways runs a cutting-edge and effective rail network that connects major cities including Tel Aviv and Jerusalem. Around an hour is needed to go by rail from Jerusalem's Yitzhak Navon station to Tel Aviv's HaHagana station. The Judean Hills are traversed by the train in comfort and beauty.

3. By Bus: Buses run frequently between Jerusalem and many Israeli cities. A significant transportation hub that serves both local and interstate services is Jerusalem's central bus terminal.

4. By Car: If you prefer to drive, you may rent a car at Ben Gurion Airport or from some Tel Aviv rental companies. You may tour Jerusalem and its surroundings at your speed if you travel there by car. But be aware that Jerusalem's traffic can be backed up, especially around rush hour.

5. By Shared Taxi (Sherut): Shared taxis, also referred to as "sheruts," are a well-liked and economical choice. They travel along a fixed route between important cities and charge set prices. Sheruts offer a shared, door-to-door service and leave once there are enough passengers.

6. By Walking: If you're already in Jerusalem or a nearby location, you have the option of exploring the Old City and city center by walking. Because Jerusalem is a relatively small city, you may explore its lively streets and distinctive ambiance on foot.

Traveling Documents

1. **Passport:** All visitors to Jerusalem must have a current passport. Verify that the expiration date of your passport is at least six months after the day you plan to travel. In case of loss or theft, it is important to carry a photocopy or digital scan of your passport in a different location.

2. **Visa:** Depending on your country of citizenship, Israel has different visa requirements. Numerous nations are entitled to visa-free entrance for brief tourist stays, including the United States, Canada, and

member states of the European Union. However, a visa may be needed in advance for some nationalities. Before visiting Jerusalem, find out if you need a visa for your country.

3. Entry Permit: In addition to your Israeli visa, you may need to get an entry permit or visa from the Palestinian Authority if you intend to travel to Bethlehem or other areas of the Palestinian territories.

4. **Return Ticket:** To enter Israel, some visitors may be required to show proof of a return or onward ticket. Make sure your departure from Israel is on a confirmed itinerary.

5. **Travel insurance** is strongly advised when visiting Jerusalem or any other international location, even though it is not a requirement for entry. It offers protection against unanticipated events like lost luggage, flight disruptions, and medical emergencies.

6. **COVID-19 Requirements:** Due to the continuing epidemic, there may be certain COVID-19-related criteria for travelers, such as displaying a negative PCR test or confirmation of immunization. Before you travel, make sure you are aware of the most recent COVID-19 entry requirements and travel advisories.

It is imperative to travel with both paper and digital copies of your travel documents. Keep your documents accessible and safe. Additionally, familiarise yourself with any security warnings or travel advisories that have been issued by your country about visits to Jerusalem and Israel.

Local Costumes and Etiquettes of the people

1. **Modest Dress:** You must wear modest clothing to visit the sacred sites in Jerusalem,

especially those in the Old City. Shoulders and knees should be covered by both men and women. In some religious settings, women may be required to cover their hair. It is advised to wear comfortable shoes because traveling through the city's winding, uneven streets.

2. **Greetings:** In the local culture, salutations are a crucial component. Men and women both commonly shake hands when meeting someone for the first time. Unless specifically requested to use their first name, use suitable titles like "Mr." or "Mrs.," followed by the person's last name.

3. **Respect at Religious Sites:** Respect the laws and regulations listed outside before entering places of worship like mosques, churches, and synagogues. To show respect for the sanctity of the places, keep voices low, avoid taking photos in sensitive locations, and dress appropriately.

4. **Public Behavior:** Because of the city's continued conservatism, couples should avoid making overt public displays of affection. A calm and respectful attitude should always be maintained, especially in busy settings and places of worship.

5. **Friday and Saturday Observance:** The Jewish Sabbath is observed from Friday evening until Saturday evening, and Saturday is the Muslim holy day. Some stores and companies may be closed or operate with limited hours during these times. Plan your activities accordingly and show respect for these religious observances.

6. **Dietary Observances:** Jerusalem has a wide variety of restaurants, but be aware of local customs and traditions. The availability of food may change during particular religious holidays, and some places may be kosher or halal.

7. **Haggling at Markets:** Bargaining is a typical practice at marketplaces, including the souks in the Old City. However, be courteous and respectful while doing so, keeping in mind the worth of the seller's items.

8. **Photography:** When photographing people, especially in contexts as private as markets or religious ceremonies, always ask for their consent.

Languages Spoken in Jerusalem

1. **Hebrew:** Hebrew is extensively spoken in Jerusalem and is Israel's official language. As the language of the Jewish people and their sacred scriptures, it is incredibly significant from both a religious and historical perspective.

2. **Arabic:** The majority of the Palestinian Arab population in Jerusalem speaks Arabic, which is another official language in Israel. For the Muslim population of the city, it is also

important because it is the language of the Quran.

3. **English:** Especially in tourist areas and among younger generations, English is widely spoken and understood. It serves as a common language for interacting with guests from other countries.

4. **Russian:** A substantial Russian-speaking community, made up of former Soviet Union immigrants and their offspring, exists in Jerusalem. In many facets of daily life and cultural activity, Russian is widely used.

5. **Yiddish:** The ultra-Orthodox (Haredi) population of some Orthodox Jewish communities in Jerusalem speaks Yiddish.

6. **French:** Due to historical ties and immigration patterns, French is a language that some populations speak, including various Jewish and Christian communities.

7. **Amharic:** Members of the Ethiopian Jewish community in Jerusalem speak Amharic.

8. **Ladino:** In Jerusalem, some Sephardic Jews speak Ladino, a Judeo-Spanish tongue.

9. **Armenian** is the language used exclusively by the Armenian population in Jerusalem.

10. **Other languages:** Due to the cosmopolitan aspect of the city, other languages can also be heard in Jerusalem, including German, Italian, Spanish, and more. This reflects the different backgrounds of the city's residents and visitors.

Phrases For Travel

When traveling to Jerusalem, knowing a few basic phrases can greatly enhance your experience and help you connect with the locals. Here are some essential phrases in English with their translations in Hebrew and Arabic:

Greetings:

1. Hello / Hi:

   - Hebrew: שָׁלוֹם (Shalom)

   - Arabic: مرحباً (Marhaban)

2. Good morning:

   - Hebrew: בוקר טוב (Boker Tov)

   - Arabic: صباح الخير (Sabah al-khayr)

3. Good evening:

   - Hebrew: ערב טוב (Erev Tov)

   - Arabic: مساء الخير (Masa' al-khayr)

Basic Expressions:

4. Please:

   - Hebrew: בבקשה (Bevakasha)

   - Arabic: من فضلك (Min fadlik)

5. Thank you:

   - Hebrew: תודה (Toda)

   - Arabic: شكراً (Shukran)

6. Yes:

   - Hebrew: כן (Ken)

   - Arabic: نعم (Na'am)

7. No:
- Hebrew: לֹא (Lo)
- Arabic: لا (La)

Getting Around:

8. Where is...?:
- Hebrew: ...?איפה נמצא (Eifo namtze...?)
- Arabic: أين يوجد...؟ (Ayna yujad...?)

9. How much is this?:
- Hebrew: כמה עולה זה? (Kama oleh ze?)
- Arabic: كم ثمن هذا؟ (Kam thaman hatha?)

10. I need a taxi:
- Hebrew: אני זקוק למונית (Ani tzarich lemonit)
- Arabic: أحتاج سيارة أجرة (Ahtaj sayyara ajrah)

Eating and Drinking:

11. Menu:
- Hebrew: תפריט (Tafrit)
- Arabic: القائمة (Al-qayimah)

12. Water:
- Hebrew: מים (Mayim)
- Arabic: ماء (Ma')

13. I would like...:

  - Hebrew: אני רוצה... (Ani rotse...)

  - Arabic: ...أود أن (Awed an...)

Emergencies:

14. Help!:

  - Hebrew: עזרה! (Ezrah!)

  - Arabic: المساعدة! (Al-musa'adah!)

15. I need a doctor:

  - Hebrew: אני זקוק לרופא (Ani tzarich le'rofe)

  - Arabic: أحتاج طبيبًا (Ahtaj tabiban)

Remember that even attempting a few phrases in the local languages can go a long way in showing respect and building connections with the people you meet during your journey in Jerusalem. The locals appreciate the effort, and it can lead to memorable and enriching experiences during your travels.

Chapter Three

Major Cities in Jerusalem

1. **Tel Aviv:** Tel Aviv is the second-largest city in Israel and a significant economic and cultural center. It is situated about 70 kilometers west of Jerusalem. Tel Aviv, which is renowned for its exciting nightlife, gorgeous beaches, and cutting-edge architecture, provides a strong contrast to Jerusalem's timeless allure.

2. **Bethlehem:** Just a few kilometers south of Jerusalem, Bethlehem is notable from a religious perspective because it is the location of Jesus Christ's birth. Sites like the Church of the Nativity are visited by pilgrims and tourists from all over the world as a result.

3. **Ramallah:** The administrative hub of the Palestinian Authority, Ramallah is situated in the West Bank, around 16 kilometers north of

Jerusalem. It is a thriving metropolis with a blend of modernism and historical culture.

4. **Jericho:** Located about 27 kilometers northeast of Jerusalem, Jericho is one of the oldest continuously inhabited cities in the world. It is home to historical and archaeological attractions like the Monastery of Temptation and the antiquated Tell es-Sultan.

5. **Haifa:** The third-largest city in Israel and a significant port, Haifa is situated about 120 km north of Jerusalem. Famous for its magnificent Bahá' Gardens and vibrant cultural scene.

6. **Jaffa (Yafo):** Located about 70 kilometers to the west of Jerusalem, Jaffa is a historic port city that is now a part of Tel Aviv-Yafo. It draws both tourists and residents with its combination of history, art, and picturesque streets.

7. **Dead Sea Resorts:** Although not actual cities, the resorts surrounding the Dead Sea, like Ein Bokek and Neve Zohar, are well-liked

stops for travelers interested in floating in the mineral-rich waters for an unforgettable experience.

Transportations

Jerusalem's main transit options are buses, taxis, and light rail. An extensive network connecting numerous communities and attractions is run by the Egged bus business. Due to their reasonable costs and regular schedules, buses are a preferred mode of transportation for both residents and visitors.

The Jerusalem Light Rail system, which travels around the city from north to south and stops at important landmarks and transport hubs, offers a more practical alternative. This environmentally friendly form of transportation has greatly increased mobility and decreased traffic.

Additionally, accessible and offering a more individualized service are taxis. For their flexibility and convenience, tourists frequently choose cabs, especially when traveling to places that are difficult to reach by other means.

Jerusalem is also very pedestrian-friendly, which encourages both locals and visitors to explore on foot. Visitors can experience the rich history and distinctive charm of the city by strolling along its winding stone streets.

Taxi

Jerusalem cabs can be located at official taxi stands or can be flagged down on the street, particularly in crowded areas and close to well-known tourist attractions. On request, most hotels can also set up transportation services for their visitors.

In Jerusalem, taxis frequently use a metered system, guaranteeing openness and reasonable pricing. To avoid any potential misunderstandings, it is suggested that you confirm the meter is running with the driver before you begin the journey.

The convenience of door-to-door service, which is especially helpful for those with limited mobility or those looking for direct routes to their destinations, is one significant benefit of using a taxi in Jerusalem. Taxis are a sensible option for late-night travel when other public transit options could have constrained timetables.

To avoid overcharging, it is crucial to have a basic sense of the expected rate for any destination. It's a good idea to inquire about an anticipated fee before beginning the ride, even though the majority of taxi drivers are trustworthy and courteous.

Car Rentals

The process of renting a car in Jerusalem is simple; the majority of companies demand a current driver's license, passport, and a certain minimum age, usually 21 or older. To guarantee availability and lock in affordable rates, it is essential to reserve a rental car in advance, especially during the busiest travel times.

Travelers can pick up their vehicles easily at Ben Gurion Airport thanks to the presence of the major car rental companies' offices at strategic places. Additionally, a lot of organizations have offices in Jerusalem's center, making it simple for visitors to get there. Some may find it difficult to maneuver through Jerusalem's winding, congested streets, but having a rental car makes it possible for tourists to travel outside of the city and into the picturesque countryside. A memorable element of the journey is the beautiful drive to adjacent locations like the Dead Sea, Bethlehem, or Masada.

To minimize any inconveniences, it is crucial to become familiar with local traffic laws and parking requirements before starting a road trip. It's a good idea to make parking arrangements in advance because some neighborhoods of Jerusalem have a shortage of parking spaces.

Chapter Four

Accommodations

Resorts and Hotels

Jerusalem offers a wide selection of opulent hotels with opulent amenities and spectacular views for those looking for luxury. These hotels guarantee a genuinely luxurious stay with rooftop pools that look out over the Old City and spa amenities that delight the senses.

As an alternative, guests might select one of the many wonderful boutique hotels hidden away in charming neighborhoods. These small-scale establishments offer individualized services and a genuine glimpse into local culture.

Budget tourists need not fret, as Jerusalem has a wide selection of reasonably priced hotels and guesthouses. These choices provide relaxing stays without sacrificing convenience or accessibility.

Resorts located outside of the city offer peace and leisure amidst natural scenery for a more immersive experience. These getaways frequently give visitors quick access to historic locations while allowing them to relax in peaceful settings.

Camping Sites

The Jerusalem Hills National Park is a well-liked camping location that offers a gorgeous environment between rolling hills and rich vegetation. Both families and lone adventurers will find it to be the ideal destination thanks to the opportunity to walk along beautiful pathways during the day and take in the stars at night.

Ein Prat Nature Reserve is a great choice for a more rural experience. It offers a tranquil retreat from the bustle of the city and is situated in the Judean Desert. The reserve has some camping places where you can pitch your tent and make friends with other campers over a fire in the desert sky.

The nearby camping area of Machtesh Ramon, which is about an hour from Jerusalem, is another excellent choice. This enormous crater offers a great setting for camping as well as several options for trekking and exploring.

It's important to respect the environment and adhere to the rules established by the park authority when camping in Jerusalem. To protect the beauty of these natural locations for future generations, don't forget to pack out any rubbish and bring the necessary camping supplies, food, and drink. Camping is fun!

Chapter Five

Religious and Historical Sites
The Western Wall Tunnels

Jerusalem's Western Wall Tunnels are a fascinating and important historical underground corridor that provides tourists with a fascinating look into the city's colorful past. These tunnels, which are found below the Western Wall, one of Judaism's holiest places, offer a fascinating tour through millennia of history.

The **tunnels**, often referred to as the "**Kotel Tunnels**," are around 485 meters long and show the layers of Jerusalem's architectural development. You'll come across relics from numerous historical eras as you go along these age-old passageways, including Second Temple-era parts, elaborate stone carvings, and old water channels.

The Western Wall Tunnels' most impressive feature is its proximity to the Holy of Holies, the Jewish Temple's innermost chamber. Worshippers travel from all over the world to this location to pray and connect with their spiritual history, and it carries great value for them.

Visitors can take advantage of guided tours that offer in-depth explanations of the site's historical and religious significance. Knowledgeable tour guides relate fascinating tales and archaeological findings, enhancing the experience and providing context.

The Western Wall Tunnels can get busy, so making reservations in advance is advised to guarantee a space on the guided tour. Wearing comfortable shoes is advised because the site requires considerable walking on rough ground.

Via Dolorosa and the Stations of the Cross

The "Way of Sorrows," also known as the Via Dolorosa, is a famous and highly renowned holy route in Jerusalem that follows the path taken by Jesus Christ on his last journey before being crucified. For millions of Christians around the world, this famous walk is of great spiritual significance and is a significant place of pilgrimage.

Each Station of the Cross along the Via Dolorosa commemorates a specific moment in Jesus' journey to Calvary. The route passes through the Old City's winding lanes before arriving at the Church of the Holy Sepulchre, which is thought to be the location of Jesus' crucifixion, burial, and resurrection. The journey starts at the Antonia Fortress, where Jesus was condemned.

Walking along this historic route, pilgrims pause to consider the immense sorrow and sacrifice that Jesus underwent. Inviting visitors to reflect on the deep significance of the events that took place here more than two millennia ago, the stations, which are identified by chapels, plaques, or straightforward markers on the walls, inspire a sense of solemnity and devotion.

The Via Dolorosa draws a large number of worshippers who join in processions and prayers along the route that Christ took during his final hours during Holy Week, notably on Good Friday.

Visitors to the Via Dolorosa can connect with their religion and follow in Jesus' footsteps, making it a very meaningful and spiritual experience. Regardless of one's beliefs, traveling down this holy pathway in the center of Jerusalem is a meaningful and unforgettable experience for everyone who does so because of its historical and cultural significance.

Mount Zion and King David's Tomb

Just outside Jerusalem's Old City walls lies a large hill known as Mount Zion, which is significant both historically and religiously. The location is well-known for holding King David's Tomb, a treasured Jewish pilgrimage site and a destination for tourists from all over the world.

King David, the well-known biblical figure and Israel's second king is said to have been buried on Mount Zion. Jews have revered the location for centuries due to its historical significance as the location of King David's tomb. Consequently, the Tomb of King David has developed into a location for prayer and contemplation, attracting both Israelis and visitors looking for a closer connection to Israel's rich history.

Beyond King David's Tomb, the location is significant from both a historical and theological standpoint. As the site of the Last Supper, a crucial moment in Jesus Christ's life, Mount Zion is also significant in the Christian tradition. Here is where Christians travel to visit the Cenacle, an upstairs room thought to be the location of the Last Supper.

While taking in breath-blowing panoramic views of Jerusalem's Old City and its famous monuments, visitors to Mount Zion can explore the Tomb of King David and the Cenacle. The site's calm environment and spiritual vibe provide a moment of rest and reflection in the busy city.

Tower of David and the Night Spectacular

Near the entrance to the Old City of Jerusalem, the Tower of David, also called the Jerusalem Citadel, rises magnificently and represents nearly 2,000 years of history. This famous building is a testament to Jerusalem's tenacity and enduring heritage because it has seen many different civilizations and historical moments.

The Tower of David, which King Herod initially built as a fortress, has had several uses throughout history, including a royal palace and a military stronghold. It now houses the Tower of David Museum, which presents the amazing history of Jerusalem through interactive exhibits and artifacts from antiquity.

The Night Spectacular is one of the Tower of David's most engaging attractions. The walls of the citadel come alive with a magnificent sound and light performance as darkness falls over the historic city. The historical occurrences and chapters that have defined Jerusalem's story are artistically portrayed in projected animations, creating a spellbinding trip through time.

The Night Spectacular interweaves the city's varied history, spanning from the biblical era and King David's reign through the rise and fall of many civilizations. The moving musical composition and fascinating visual storytelling transport the audience into Jerusalem's past, inspiring a deep sense of awe and connection to the city's colorful past.

The Tower of David's impressive architecture and the captivating Night Spectacular together provide visitors with a truly immersive and life-changing experience. For those who want to explore Jerusalem's rich history and experience the enduring spirit of this ageless city, it is a must-visit site.

Al-Aqsa Mosque and Islamic Heritage

One of the holiest places in the Muslim world, Al-Aqsa Mosque is located in Jerusalem's Old City and has great significance for Islamic heritage.

Millions of Muslims hold this revered mosque in the highest regard, and both worshippers and outsiders are drawn to its sanctified grounds.

Al-Aqsa Mosque's history is extensive and varied. The Prophet Muhammad is said to have been magically transported there during the Night Journey, rising to the heavens to meet with God and the forerunner prophets, according to Islamic tradition. As a result, the mosque is of great spiritual significance and is a popular place for Muslims looking to strengthen their religion and get closer to God.

In addition to having religious significance, the Al-Aqsa Mosque is a masterpiece of exquisite architecture. Its eye-catching golden dome, graceful arches, and exquisite mosaics are proof of the creativity of Islamic workmanship throughout the ages. Thousands of worshippers can fit in the spacious courtyard and prayer halls, making it a thriving hub for group prayer and spiritual meetings.

In addition to the mosque itself, the entire Al-Aqsa Mosque Compound, also known as Haram al-Sharif, is of immeasurable historical significance. It includes the well-known Dome of the Rock, a marvel of architecture that is cherished by Muslims and esteemed by people from all over the world.

Beyond mere religious significance, the Al-Aqsa Mosque Compound serves as a representation of Jerusalem's complicated and intertwined history, highlighting the common roots of Judaism, Christianity, and Islam.

Visitors get the chance to experience the beauty of Islamic art, the profundity of Muslim spirituality, and the significance of this location in fostering interfaith understanding and conversation by touring the Al-Aqsa Mosque and its surrounding area.

It is still a location where Jerusalem's Islamic heritage continues to flourish, luring people from all walks of life to engage with the diverse cultural heritage of this historic city.

Chapter Six

Outdoor Adventures

Hiking in and Around Jerusalem

The Jerusalem Hills are among the most well-liked places for trekking close to Jerusalem. Some marked trails weave through lush valleys, historic olive trees, and lovely villages in this picturesque region. For instance, the Mount Sorek route offers tranquility away from the hustle and bustle of the city and leads to breathtaking overlooks overlooking the area.

The Judaean Desert, with its arid scenery and intriguing geological formations, calls for a more adventurous walk. Many trails lead to cool waterfalls and desert oases in the Ein Gedi Nature Reserve, which is near the Dead Sea. A very compelling experience is created by the stark contrast between the desert and the blue waters of the Dead Sea.

Hikers have the opportunity to discover historic sites in addition to the surrounding natural beauty. A strenuous climb or cable car ride will take you to the ancient fortress of Masada, which provides a fascinating look into Jewish history and resistance.

The Jerusalem Trail offers an urban hiking experience within the city, weaving past parks, communities, and famous sites. The route links contemporary Jerusalem to its historical roots by passing through important cultural landmarks like the Old City walls and Mount of Olives.

Ein Hemed National Park

Ein Hemed National Park is a hidden gem that provides tourists with a lovely getaway into the peace of nature. It is located right in the middle of Jerusalem. This park, also known as "Aqua Bella" or "Ein Hemed Spring," is a tranquil sanctuary of lush foliage, ancient ruins, and cooling springs that is a popular refuge for both locals and visitors looking for a tranquil setting. The Ein Hemed Spring, which supplies a tranquil pool encircled by antiquated stone walls and arched bridges, is the park's main draw. A fantastic location for leisure and picnics is created by the towering trees' shade and the calming sound of water flowing over rocks.

Hikers and nature lovers will enjoy exploring the park's well-maintained trails, which meander alongside the seasonally flowing stream and weave through forested regions. For those who enjoy nature and photography, the lush environment offers many possibilities to explore the native flora and fauna.

The Crusader ruins that dot the landscape are proof that Ein Hemed National Park has historical value in addition to its natural beauty. The ruins of a medieval stronghold and a splendid Crusader cathedral give the park an air of mystery and intrigue that appeals to history buffs and people who are curious about the area's past.

The park often holds festivals, concerts, and cultural events that enhance the visiting experience and give a glimpse of Jerusalem's thriving arts and culture scene.

Desert Excursions

Masada National Park is one of the must-see locations for desert vacations. The famous Masada stronghold is located at this UNESCO World Heritage Site, positioned atop a breathtaking cliff. The peak of the mountain, which may be reached by hiking up the Snake Path, offers breathtaking views of the Dead Sea and the surrounding desert.

A trip to the Dead Sea is essential for a restorative and renewing experience. The Dead Sea is the lowest place on Earth, and because of its high salt content, visitors can float gently on its buoyant waves. Mineral-rich mud found near the sea offers spa-like natural treatments that revitalize the skin.

Ein Gedi Nature Reserve is a wonderful desert treasure for those with a spirit of adventure. There are waterfalls, luxuriant foliage, and undiscovered springs in this arid oasis. Its hiking trails offer a chance to view wildlife, such as ibexes and different bird species.

The Ramon Crater, also known as Makhtesh Ramon, is a fascinating geological phenomenon located further south. This enormous crater is a favorite destination for astronomy aficionados and stargazers since it exhibits unusual rock formations and offers unmatched viewing chances at night.

For desert excursions, guided tours are offered, allowing guests to learn from professional guides about the region's geological and historical significance. The desert excursions in Jerusalem can be tailored to suit a variety of interests and inclinations, from exhilarating 4×4 safaris to serene sunset camel rides.

Chapter Seven

Sightseeing

Ancient Monuments

The **Western Wall** sometimes referred to as the Wailing Wall, is one of Jerusalem's most recognisable ancient structures. This holy location is a destination of prayer, reflection, and pilgrimage for Jews because it was once a portion of the Second Temple's retaining wall.

Another magnificent historical structure is **the Dome of the Rock**, which is situated on the Temple Mount. This magnificent golden-domed building, a masterpiece of Islamic architecture, is revered by Muslims as the location of the Prophet Muhammad's purported ascent to paradise during the Night Journey.

The Church of the Holy Sepulchre,

A notable Christian pilgrimage site is the Church of the Holy Sepulchre, which is located in the Old City's Christian Quarter. It is one of the holiest sites in Christianity since it is thought to include the locations of Jesus' crucifixion, burial, and resurrection.

The Tower of David, commonly referred to as the Jerusalem Citadel, is a historic fortress that has been around for almost 2,000 years. It now serves as the home of the Tower of David Museum, which features exhibitions and artifacts from the city's ancient heritage.

Jerusalem is brimming with archaeological monuments, like the City of David, the Cardo, and the Pool of Bethesda, that provide a look into the city's ancient past and the life of its former residents. These sites are in addition to the city's well-known landmarks.

It is like traveling back in time to explore Jerusalem's historic sites, which provides a rich appreciation for the city's layers of history and the significance it has for various cultures and religions. They entice visitors to immerse themselves in the compelling story of Jerusalem's ageless legacy by acting as a link between the past and the present.

Museums

One of Jerusalem's most notable cultural institutions, **the Israel Museum** is home to a sizable collection of objects that date back thousands of years. There are archaeological artifacts, Jewish ceremonial items, and an amazing replica of Jerusalem during the Second Temple era among its exhibits. Modern sculptures and installations are displayed in the museum's large outdoor Art Garden, which brings a contemporary element to the museum's historically accurate surroundings.

Yad Vashem is a serious and moving memorial and museum for individuals who are interested in the Holocaust. It honors the six million Jewish Holocaust victims and chronicles the horrific tales of the surviving using personal items, testimony, and records from the past. Yad Vashem's dedication to commemoration and education guarantees that future generations will learn from the mistakes of the past.

The robust cultural landscape in Jerusalem will excite art lovers, with institutions like the Israel Museum's Billy Rose Art Garden, the Jerusalem Artists' House, and the L.A. The Mayer Museum for Islamic Art houses a variety of artistic works from various historical and geographic contexts.

The history of Jerusalem is brought to life through multimedia exhibits and immersive displays at **the Tower of David Museum**, which is housed within the historic fortress. While learning about the city's colorful past, visitors can tour the citadel's numerous chambers and walls.

Jerusalem's museums include a wide range of subjects, not just historical and aesthetic ones. For inquiring minds of all ages, the Bloomfield Science Museum offers engaging educational activities that make science approachable and fun for everyone.

Shopping

There are numerous markets around Jerusalem's Old City, each with a unique character. A sensory delight, the busy Arab Shuk (market) is lined with vendors offering spices, jewelry, fabrics, and traditional handicrafts. The joy of buying is increased by the frequent practice of haggling here.

The Christian Quarter and Jewish Quarter both include a variety of stores offering religious icons, prayer shawls, mezuzahs, and other sacrosanct objects for those looking for religious souvenirs. These keepsakes offer a deep link to the city's extensive spiritual tradition.

In the city's modern retail centers, one may experience the current side of shopping. A sophisticated and cosmopolitan atmosphere is created by the luxury boutiques, worldwide brands, and trendy cafes found in the Mamilla Mall, which is immediately beyond the Jaffa Gate.

The numerous galleries and art studios located all across Jerusalem provide a refuge for art enthusiasts and collectors.

These venues feature the works of regional artists and offer the chance to bring a piece of Jerusalem's thriving art scene home.

For foodies, the Mahane Yehuda Market, popularly referred to as "The Shuk," is a must-visit. This vibrant marketplace offers a genuine flavor of the city's culinary delights with its abundance of fresh vegetables, spices, artisanal cheeses, and mouthwatering street cuisine.

Visiting Jerusalem's shopping areas is more than just a chance to buy stuff; it's also a chance to engage with the city's rich culture, meet residents, and enjoy the distinctive atmosphere of this old yet modern metropolis.

Chapter Eight

Food and Drinks

Restaurants

The Arab Quarter in the Old City and Mahane Yehuda Market are two places you must go if you want to sample genuine regional cuisine. These crowded sections are home to falafel shops, shawarma restaurants, and hummus bars that serve mouthwatering street cuisine.

A wide range of fine dining establishments can be found in Machane Yehuda Market, where chefs create modern culinary delights using products that are procured locally. The vibrant energy of the market adds yet another level of enjoyment to the dining experience.

A more upmarket dining experience can be found in the German Colony and Emek Refaim Street neighborhoods, which are home to quaint cafés and restaurants providing food from throughout the world. You can have delectable steaks, French croissants, and Italian spaghetti here.

Restaurants that follow Jewish dietary regulations and are kosher should be tried if you want to experience a immersive culinary trip. Explore the carefully and precisely made traditional Jewish foods at these establishments.

Visitors who are vegetarian or vegan need not be concerned, as Jerusalem has an increasing number of plant-based restaurants that cater to people with dietary restrictions and environmental awareness.

Jerusalem's restaurant scene has it all, whether you're looking for a cozy family-friendly setting, a romantic evening with rooftop views, or an eclectic fusion of flavors.

The city's diverse cuisine is a product of its multiculturalism and a testament to its prominence as a top travel destination for foodies worldwide.

Local Cuisines

Jerusalem's regional cuisine is inextricably linked to the mouthwatering variety of Middle Eastern foods. Every tourist should eat hummus, a beloved delicacy made from chickpeas, tahini, and olive oil and served with warm pita bread. Another well-liked street snack is falafel, deep-fried chickpea balls that are flavored with herbs and spices and have a pleasing crunch.

Whether cooked with lamb, chicken, or beef, delectable kebabs are a tantalizing option for meat eaters. These flavorful skewers are seasoned with savory rice and aromatic vegetables that have been barbecued.

Jerusalem's cuisine is especially fond of the traditional Palestinian dish makluba. Rice, meat (usually chicken or lamb), and veggies are cooked together in this one-pot miracle, which is then turned upside down when it's time to serve to create a delicious and aesthetically pleasing dish.

The rich culinary tradition of the Jews is reflected in the distinctive cuisine of Jerusalem. Popular traditional breakfast options include Shakshuka, a savory tomato and egg dish frequently spiced with paprika and cumin.

The myriad of sweet delights offered is yet another example of the city's diverse ethnicities. Jerusalem's dessert selections are likely to satisfy any sweet craving, from baklava, a flaky pastry packed with nuts and sweet syrup, to kanafeh, a cheese-based confection drenched in fragrant rose water.

Visit lively markets or local family-run restaurants for a genuine cultural experience, where the aroma of freshly made food fills the air. Embracing the unique cuisine of Jerusalem means immersing oneself in the culture and history of the city as well as enjoying the flavors.

Local Drinks

"Sahlab," a warming winter beverage, is one that you must try. Infused with cinnamon and almonds, this creamy, spiced milk-based mixture is prepared from powdered orchid root and offers a calming and pleasant experience. During the colder months, it is a cherished favorite that warms the hearts of people who drink it.

Locals frequently enjoy "limonana," a fiery concoction of lemonade and mint, for a cool twist. This refreshing beverage offers a burst of zesty flavor with a tinge of cooling mint, making it the ideal companion on a sweltering summer day.

Raise a glass of "arak" for those desiring a traditional alcoholic beverage. Arak is a potent anise-flavored liquor that is frequently diluted with water to create a milky white elixir that is best consumed slowly while having a meal or conversation.

Street Foods

Nothing surpasses the famed "falafel" for a quick and savory feast. These deep-fried chickpea balls are crispy on the exterior and tender on the inside, served on warm pita bread with a variety of fresh veggies and creamy tahini sauce. The flavor explosion that occurs with the first bite makes falafel one of Jerusalem's must-try street foods.

Sabich, a delicious sandwich made with fried eggplant, hard-boiled eggs, Israeli salad, and a drizzle of amba sauce originating from Iraqi-Jewish cuisine, is another well-known local treat. Sabich is a dish that perfectly encapsulates Jerusalem's rich culinary tradition with its variety of flavors and textures.

The delicious delicacy known as "rugelach," which is based on Eastern European Jewish customs, is perfect for anyone with a sweet craving. The various sweet fillings inside these crescent-shaped delights, including chocolate, cinnamon, and fruit preserves, provide a wonderful explosion of flavors with each bite.

You'll be drawn in by the aroma of freshly baked "Jerusalem bagels" as you stroll through Jerusalem's picturesque streets. These oval-shaped treats, which differ from typical bagels in that they are sprinkled with sesame seeds, are deliciously crispy and ideal for dipping into creamy spreads like labneh or za'atar.

Chapter Nine

Safety and Health

Vaccinations

Vaccinations for regular diseases such as measles, mumps, rubella (MMR), diphtheria, tetanus, pertussis (DTaP), polio, and varicella (chickenpox) should be current. No matter where they are going, all travelers need to get these basic immunizations.

Hepatitis A: Because it can spread through tainted food and water, you should think about getting immunized. If you want to experience the local cuisine or travel to places with few sanitary facilities, you need to take extra precautions.

Hepatitis B: A vaccination against Hepatitis B is advised for tourists who may come into close contact with natives or who may need medical attention while visiting.

Typhoid: Getting vaccinated against typhoid is advised if you plan to consume street food or travel to remote locations because it is frequently spread through tainted food and water.

Rabies: Getting vaccinated against rabies is a wise precaution for anyone who intends to interact with animals or participate in outdoor activities like trekking.

To receive individualized guidance based on your medical history and travel plans, speak with a travel health expert or your doctor well in advance of your trip. To further guarantee a secure and happy trip to Jerusalem, keep in mind to practice excellent hygiene, drink bottled water, and be cautious when eating.

Dealing with Emergencies

Know Important Emergency Contacts: Get to know important emergency contacts, such as your local police department (100), the hospital (101 or 120), and the embassy or consulate of your nation. In case your phone runs out of battery, save these numbers on your phone and save a printed copy as well.

Jerusalem is generally a safe city, but in case of any disturbance or security issues, be aware of the present situation and keep up with local news reports. If necessary, take refuge in your home or any other place that has been recognized as safe.

Medical care: In the event of an emergency, go to the closest hospital or clinic. It's a good idea to obtain travel insurance that, in the event of an emergency, covers medical costs, including repatriation.

Language assistance: Although Hebrew and Arabic, the two official languages of the area, are widely spoken, it can be useful to know a few basic words in English to communicate in an emergency.

Stay Alert and Calm: In the event of any emergency, remain composed and use good judgment. Pay attention to local authorities' recommendations and steer clear of potentially dangerous circumstances.

Inform Others: If you're traveling alone, let someone know your schedule and daily destinations. Keep in touch frequently with your friends and family back home. Natural catastrophes: Although they are uncommon, it's wise to be prepared for eventual catastrophes like earthquakes. Make sure you are familiar with the emergency protocols and escape routes at your lodging.

Avoid Political Gatherings: Exercise caution when near protests or political events. Even though they are frequently quiet, they can abruptly worsen.

You may reduce hazards and have a safe and enjoyable experience in Jerusalem by being informed, taking the appropriate safety measures, and being aware of your surroundings. Keep in mind that the city's great hospitality extends to helping guests during trying times, so don't be afraid to ask for assistance if necessary.

Conclusion

As we reach the end of **The Updated Jerusalem Travel Guide 2023-2024**, we hope your journey through this captivating city has been nothing short of extraordinary. Jerusalem, with its kaleidoscope of history, spirituality, and cultural wonders, has likely left an indelible mark on your heart and soul.

Throughout this guide, we have endeavored to showcase the essence of Jerusalem, providing you with a comprehensive and immersive experience. From the hallowed grounds of the Old City to the vibrant neighborhoods of modern Jerusalem, each step was an opportunity to unearth the city's secrets and embrace its unique tapestry of life.

You've marveled at the majesty of the Western Wall, feeling the weight of centuries of prayers and dreams echoed in its ancient stones. You've been awe-struck by the ethereal beauty of the Dome of the Rock, standing as a symbol of Jerusalem's spiritual significance to millions around the world.

Beyond the historical and religious splendor, you've indulged in Jerusalem's diverse flavors, tantalizing your taste buds with sumptuous dishes and learning how food is more than just sustenance—it's a celebration of culture and heritage.

We hope that this guide has not only been a roadmap for your exploration but a catalyst for meaningful connections with the people who call Jerusalem home. The city's warmth and hospitality are as integral to its identity as its ancient landmarks, and we trust that you've felt the embrace of its open arms.

As you return home, carry with you the stories you've uncovered, the friendships you've forged, and the awe-inspiring moments that have touched your spirit. Let the experiences you've gathered inspire you to be an ambassador for Jerusalem's enduring legacy, sharing its tale with those around you and fostering a deeper understanding of this remarkable city.

Remember, the 2023-2024 edition of The Jerusalem Travel Guide may have come to an end, but Jerusalem's story continues to unfold with each passing day. We encourage you to return and discover how the city evolves, yet always remains true to its heritage.

We appreciate you joining us on this adventure. Your exploration of Jerusalem is a testament to the unyielding power of travel, fostering connections and transcending borders to unite us all as global citizens.

Farewell, and until we meet again in the timeless city of Jerusalem.

With heartfelt gratitude.

The Updated Jerusalem Travel Guide 2023-2024

Printed in Great Britain
by Amazon

27956119R00050